SEA CREATURES

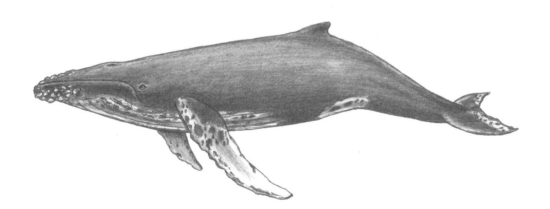

How2DrawAnimals

T0014715

Brimming with creative inspiration, how-to projects, and useful information to enrich your everyday life, quarto.com is a favorite destination for those pursuing their interests and passions.

© 2022 Quarto Publishing Group USA Inc.
Illustrations and text © 2022 P. Mendoza

First published in 2022 by Walter Foster Jr., an imprint of The Quarto Group.
100 Cummings Center, Suite 265D, Beverly, MA 01915, USA.
T (978) 282-9590 **F** (978) 283-2742 **www.quarto.com** • **www.walterfoster.com**

Walter Foster Jr. titles are also available at discount for retail, wholesale, promotional, and bulk purchase. For details, contact the Special Sales Manager by email at specialsales@quarto.com or by mail at The Quarto Group, Attn: Special Sales Manager, 100 Cummings Center, Suite 265D, Beverly, MA 01915, USA.

ISBN: 978-0-7603-8080-2

Digital edition published in 2022
eISBN: 978-0-7603-8081-9

Printed in China
10 9 8 7 6 5 4 3

TABLE OF CONTENTS

TOOLS & MATERIALS

Welcome! You don't need much to start learning how to draw. Anyone can draw with just a pencil and piece of scrap paper, but if you want to get more serious about your art, additional artist's supplies are available.

PAPER If you choose printer paper, buy a premium paper that is thick enough and bright. Portable sketch pads keep all your drawings in one place, which is convenient. For more detailed art pieces, use a fine art paper.

PENCILS Standard No. 2 pencils and mechanical pencils are great to start with and inexpensive. Pencils with different graphite grades can be very helpful when shading because a specific grade (such as 4H, 2B, or HB) will only get so dark.

PENCIL SHARPENER Electric sharpeners are faster than manual ones, but they also wear down pencils faster. It's most economical to use an automatic one for inexpensive pencils and a manual sharpener for expensive ones.

ERASERS Some erasers can smear, bend, and even tear your paper, so get a good one that erases cleanly without smudges. Kneaded erasers are pliable and can be molded for precise erasing. They leave no residue, and they last a long time.

PENS If you want to outline a drawing after sketching it, you can use a regular Sharpie® pen or marker. For more intricate pieces, try Micron® pens, which come in a variety of tip thicknesses.

DRAWING BASICS

How to Draw Shapes

For the first steps of each project in this book, you will be drawing basic shapes as guide lines. Use light, smooth strokes and don't press down too hard with your pencil. If you sketch lightly at first, it will be easier to erase if you make a mistake.

You'll be drawing a lot of circles, which many beginning artists find difficult to create. These circles do not have to be perfect because they are just guides, but if you want to practice making better circles, try the four-marks method, as shown below.

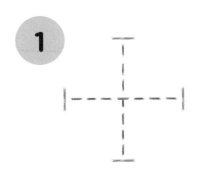

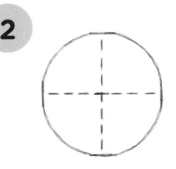

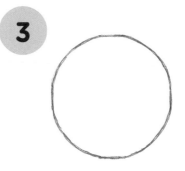

Mark where you want the top of the circle and, directly below, make another mark for the bottom. Do the same for the sides of the circle. If it helps, lightly draw a dotted line to help you place the other mark.

Once you have the four marks spaced apart equally, connect them using curved lines.

Erase any dotted lines you created, and you have a circle!

ADDITIONAL SHAPES While circles are usually what people find the most challenging, there are many other lines and shapes that you should practice and master. An arc can become a muzzle or tongue. Triangles can be ears, teeth, or claws. A football shape can become an eye. A curvy line can make a tail and an angled line a leg. Study the animal and note the shapes that stand out to you.

How to Shade

The final step to drawing an animal is to add shading so that it looks three-dimensional, and then adding texture so that it looks furry, feathery, smooth, or scaly. To introduce yourself to shading, follow the steps below.

1

Understand your pencil with a value scale. Using any pencil, start to shade lightly on one side and gradually darken your strokes toward the other side. This value scale will show you how light and dark your pencil can be.

2

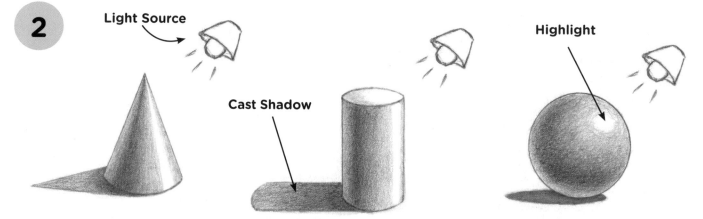

Apply the value scale to simple shapes. Draw simple shapes and shade them to make them look three-dimensional. Observe shadows in real life. Study how the light interacts with simple objects and creates shadows. Then try drawing what you see.

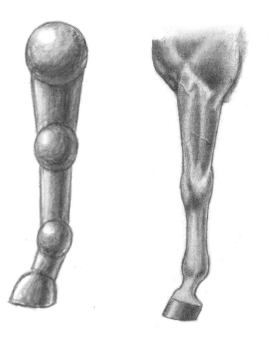

3

Practice with more complex objects. Once you're comfortable shading simple objects, move on to more complex ones. Note, for example, how a horse's leg is made up of cylinders and spheres. Breaking down your subject into simple shapes makes it easier to visualize the shadows.

How to Add Texture

Take what you've learned about shading one step further by adding texture to your drawings.

FURRY

One quick pencil stroke creates a single hair. Keep adding more quick, short strokes and you'll get a furry texture. Separate each individual stroke a bit so that the white of the paper comes through.

Create stripes and patterns by varying the pressure on your pencil to get different degrees of tonal value.

Make sure that your strokes follow the forms of the animal. As you shade a furry animal, use strokes that go in the general direction of the fur growth. The fur here follows the form of a simple sphere.

 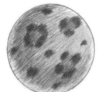

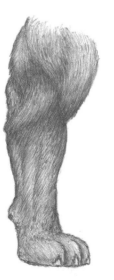

This is how to add fur to a complex form, which is easier if you know the animal's anatomy. In order to show the muscle structure, this image shows an exaggerated example of a lion's front leg and paw.

SMOOTH

For very short fur or smooth skin, add graphite evenly. Blend with a cotton swab, blending stump, or piece of tissue if needed.

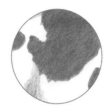

SCALY

For scaly animals like reptiles or dragons, create each individual scale with a tiny arc. Then add shadows to make the form look three-dimensional.

For a much easier way to get a scaly look, just add a bunch of squiggles! Make the squiggles darker in areas of pattern, as well as when adding shadows.

FEATHERED When adding texture to feathered animals, approach it as you would with fur or with smooth skin. Use a series of short strokes for fine or fluffy feathers. For smooth feathers, use even, blended value.

DOLPHIN

1

Lightly sketch three circles on your page. These are guides to help you create the head and body of the dolphin. Pay attention to the size and placement of each circle. These first steps are important because if you place them too far apart, your dolphin will be too long. Too close and the dolphin will be short.

2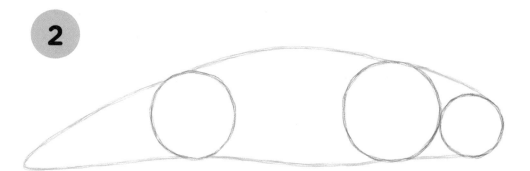

Connect the three circles with curved lines, and add a triangular shape on the left.

3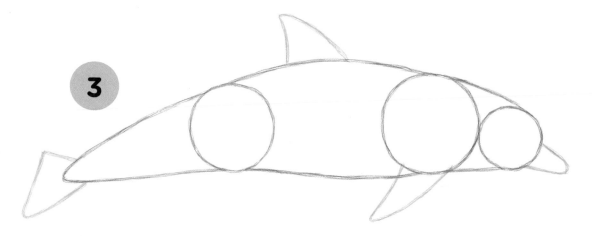

Finish up your guide lines by adding guides for the snout, flippers, dorsal fin, and tail flukes.

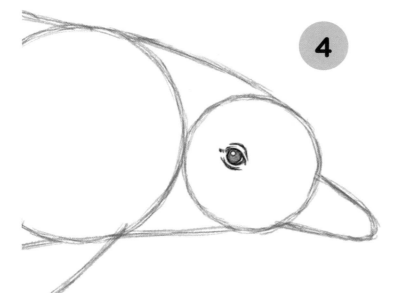

4

Draw the eye and shade it in, leaving a small circle unshaded to represent a highlight. Draw a few lines around the eye for extra detail.

5

Complete the rostrum, which is what the beak-like mouth area on a dolphin is called. Draw the mouth as a line that ends near the eye, and add curved lines to complete the top and bottom part of the rostrum.

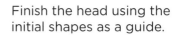

6

Finish the head using the initial shapes as a guide.

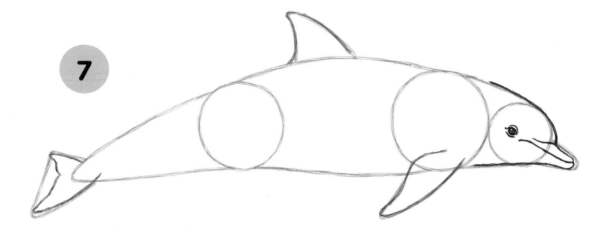

7

Using curved lines for a more natural, organic look, draw the dorsal fin on the top, the flipper at the bottom near the head, and the flukes at the back.

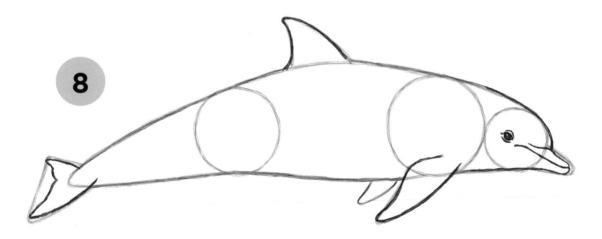

8

Use the remaining lines as guides to draw the rest of the body. Simply darken the outer lines to create that sleek, slender dolphin shape. Don't forget to add the visible portion of the flipper that's on the other side of the body.

9

For a cleaner look, erase as much as you can of the initial guide lines. Don't worry about erasing all of them. It's okay to leave some behind. Also re-draw any of the final lines you may have accidentally erased.

10

Add some shading to make your dolphin look more three-dimensional. Vary the pressure on your pencil to get different degrees of tonal value. Note the areas of light and dark in the reference image and try to create that on your drawing. The blank streaks on the body are highlights that make the dolphin look smooth and shiny.

SEA LION

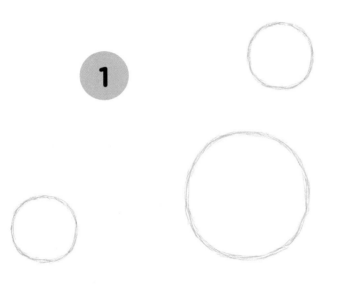

1 Lightly sketch three circles as a guide for the body and head.

2 Create the body, add an arc on the head as a guide for the muzzle, and add three angled lines under the body for the flippers.

3

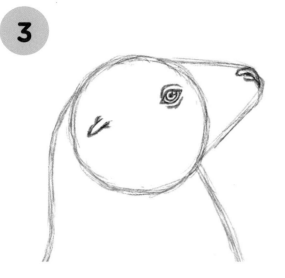

Draw the eye shape, which is similar to a football. Inside, draw a circle for the eyeball, a tiny highlight circle, and the pupil. Add a few extra lines around the eye for wrinkles. Then draw the nose on the tip of the muzzle and a small ear on the upper left side of the head.

4

Use the initial guides to draw the rest of the muzzle and head. Add lines for the mouth and folds in the skin on the neck.

Draw the first flipper. The base starts inside the body circle, and the shape of the flipper bends to the left outside of the body. Draw a few lines at the end of the flipper for extra detail.

5

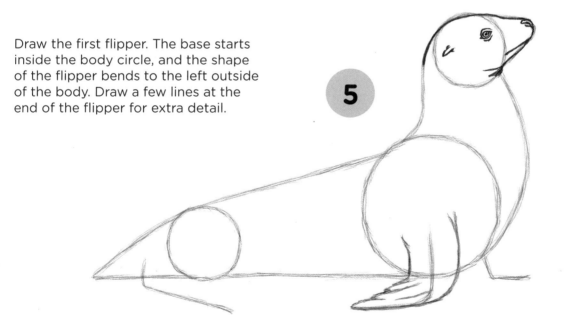

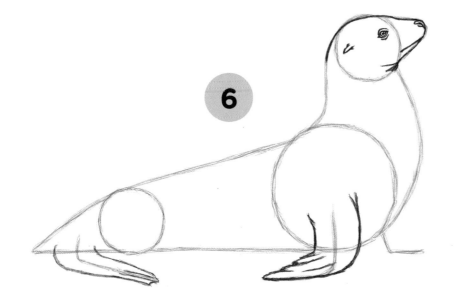

6

The hind flipper is similar to the front.

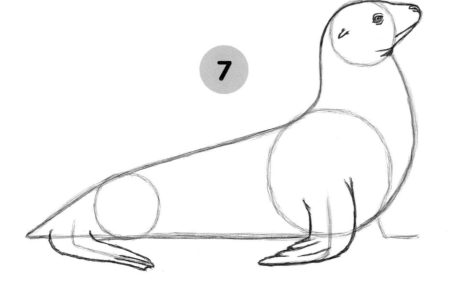

7

Draw the rest of the body by using the remaining lines as guides. The small nub on the left makes the tail.

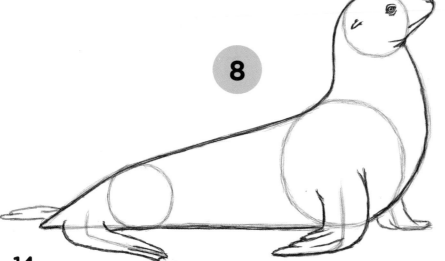

8

Finally, draw the visible portions of the flippers on the other side of the body.

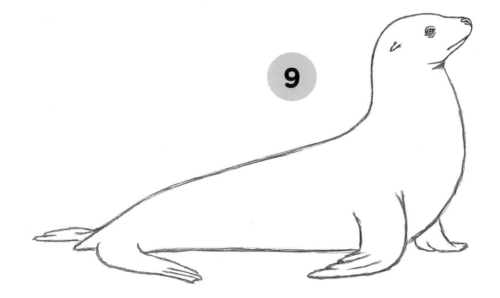

9

For a cleaner look, erase as much as you can of the initial guide lines. Don't worry about erasing all of the guides. It's okay to leave some behind. Also re-draw any final sketch lines that you may have accidentally erased.

Add some shading to your drawing to give it more dimension and volume, and add a cast shadow underneath. Then add more value throughout your drawing for extra detail. Leave a portion of the body in the middle unshaded to give the sea lion a shiny, wet look.

10

CAST SHADOWS If a sea creature isn't swimming in your drawing, add a cast shadow underneath it. This will help ground the animal so it doesn't appear to be floating. Use a darker value near the middle of the shadow and a lighter value along the edge.

CLOWNFISH

Draw a circle and add an arc on the right and left sides to create a shape that looks kind of like an eye.

1

2

Add the fins and tail using arc shapes. You now have all of the guide lines, so you can move on to adding the details in the next step!

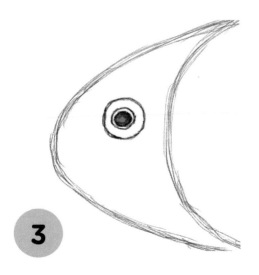

3

Draw the eye as a filled-in circle with two additional circles around it.

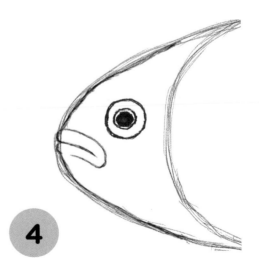

4

Draw the down-turned mouth using curved lines. Finish the head by darkening the initial arc as a guide.

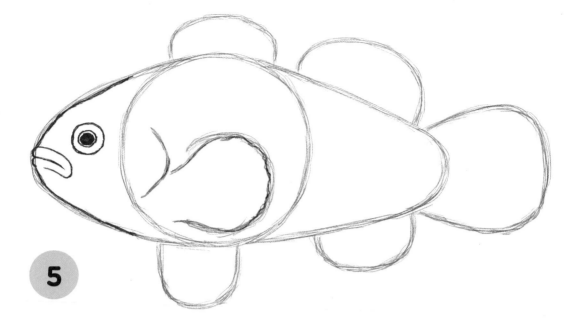

5

Create the pectoral fin by following the basic path of the backward C shape in the body and making the line wavier. Draw a curved line to the left of the pectoral fin for the gill cover.

6

Use the two arcs on the top as guides to draw the dorsal fin. The dorsal fin is one long fin that dips in the middle, giving the illusion of two fins. Make the lines wavier as you darken them. Then use the arcs on the bottom to draw the lower fins.

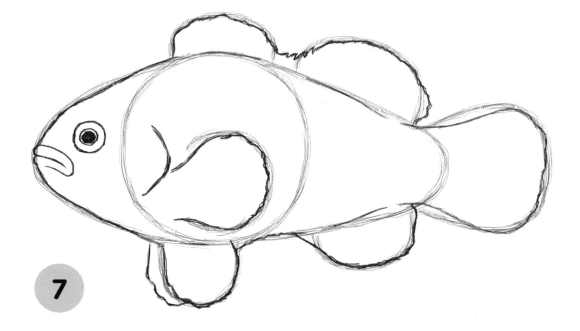

7

Use the remaining shapes and lines as guides to draw the rest of the body and tail. Add the visible part of the fin that's on the other side of the body.

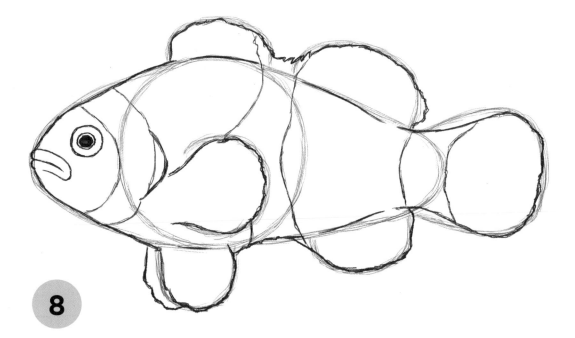

8

Draw the trademark clownfish pattern using a series of curved lines along the body. The first white band goes between the eye and the gill. The second is in the middle, behind the pectoral fin. The final band is on the right just before the tail.

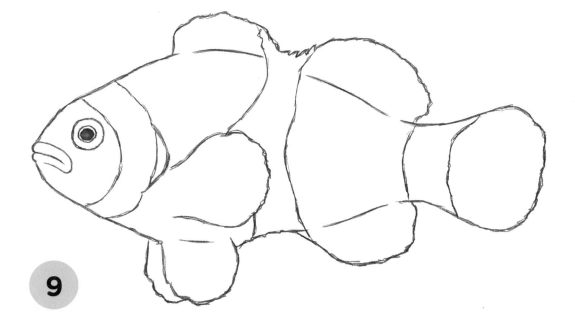

9

Stop here for a sketch or erase guide lines and tidy up your drawing before shading. You could also try coloring this bright fish with orange and black colored pencils or markers.

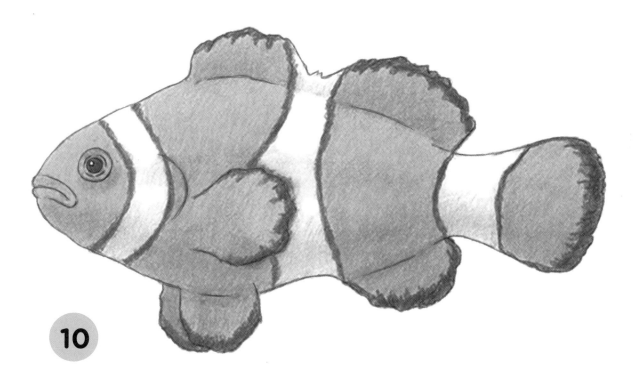

10

Add some shading to give the clownfish more dimension and volume. Add light value in the shadowed parts of the white bands, a medium value on the rest of the body, and dark value on the black fin edges and in the eye.

GREAT WHITE SHARK

1 Lightly sketch two circles on your paper, which will help you draw the body and head in the next step.

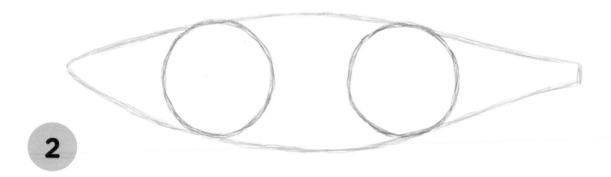

2 Draw a triangle-like shape on the left for the head and the right for the tail. Connect the two circles for the body.

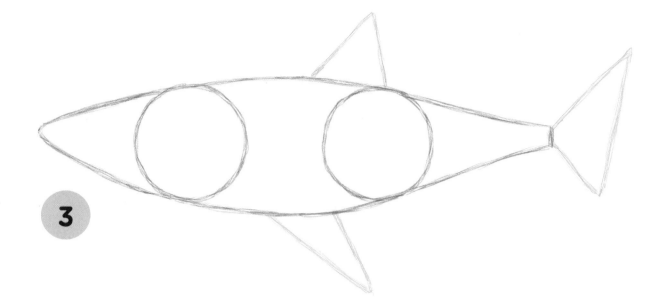

3

Complete the guide lines by adding triangle shapes for the dorsal fin on the top, pectoral fin on the bottom, and the tail or caudal fin on the right.

GUIDE LINES Remember to sketch in guide lines lightly, and don't worry if your circles aren't perfect. Turn back to page 5 to refresh your memory on how to draw a circle. You will erase guide lines later on, so instead of worrying about making a perfect circle, focus more on its size and placement in relation to the rest of the shapes.

4

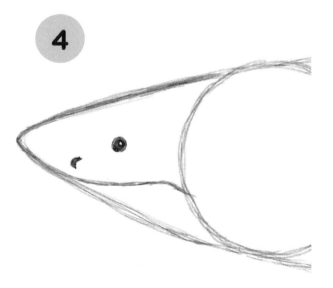

Make a small circle for the shark's eye and shade it in. Then draw a small, curved line for the nose, and fill in the top of the shark's head and mouth.

5

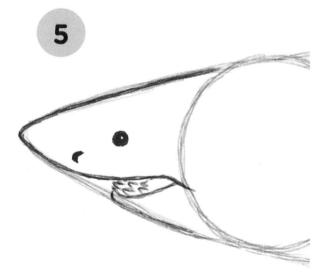

Add the lower jaw and rows of tiny triangles for the teeth.

6

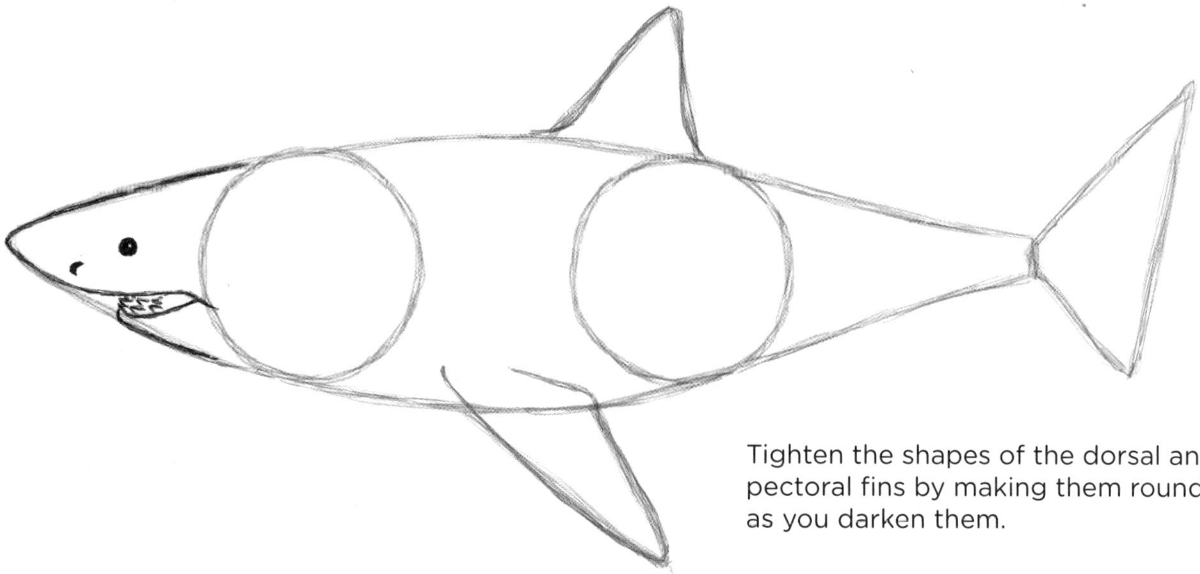

Tighten the shapes of the dorsal and pectoral fins by making them rounder as you darken them.

7

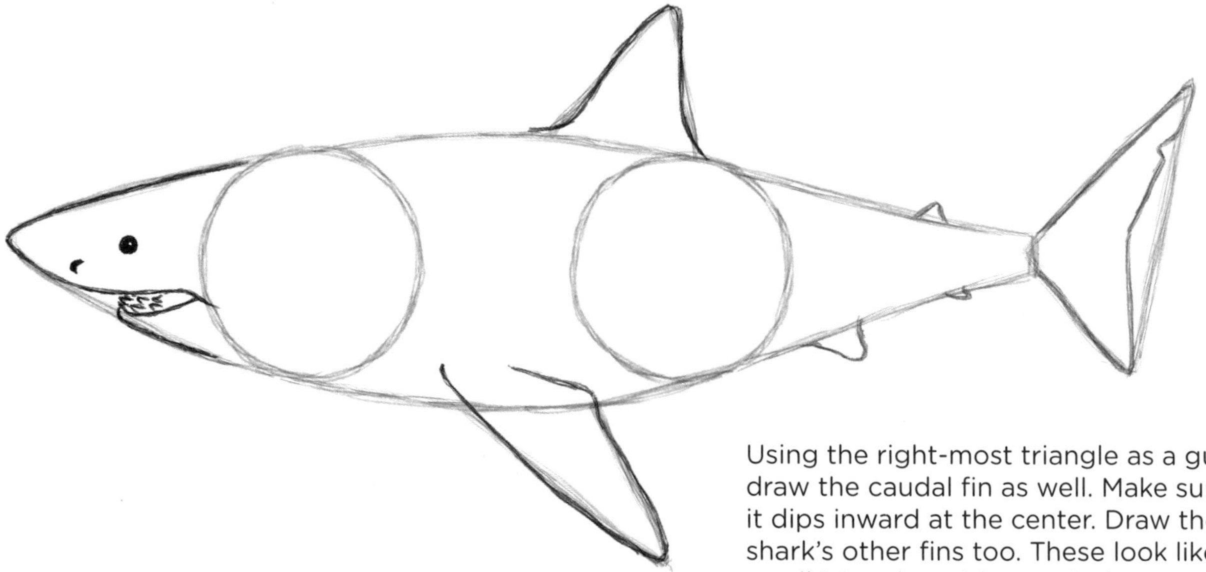

Using the right-most triangle as a guide, draw the caudal fin as well. Make sure it dips inward at the center. Draw the shark's other fins too. These look like small triangles with rounded tops.

8

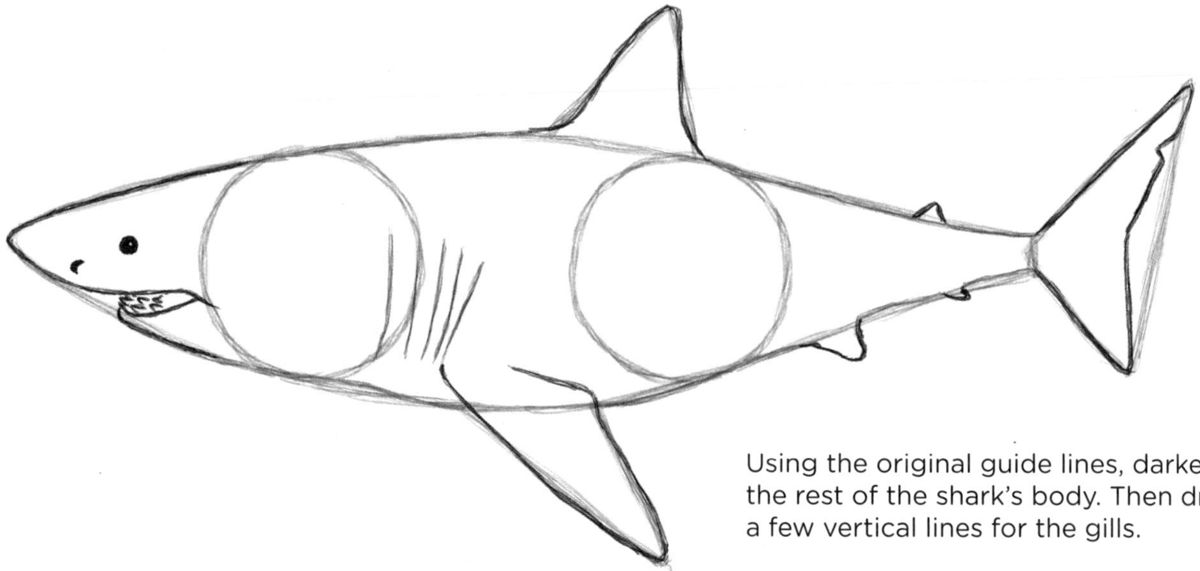

Using the original guide lines, darken in the rest of the shark's body. Then draw a few vertical lines for the gills.

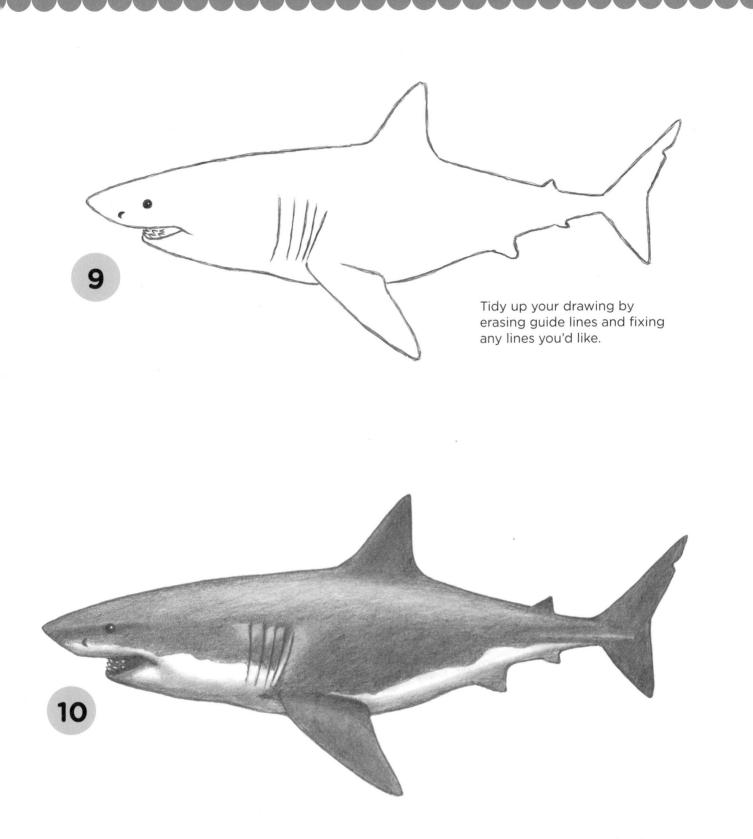

9 Tidy up your drawing by erasing guide lines and fixing any lines you'd like.

10

Draw a wavy line across the body to represent the shark's countershading (the split in color from the top and bottom). Add value to the top and leave the bottom white, but add some shading to give your shark more dimension and volume. Leave a portion near the top of the body very light or unshaded to represent underwater sheen.

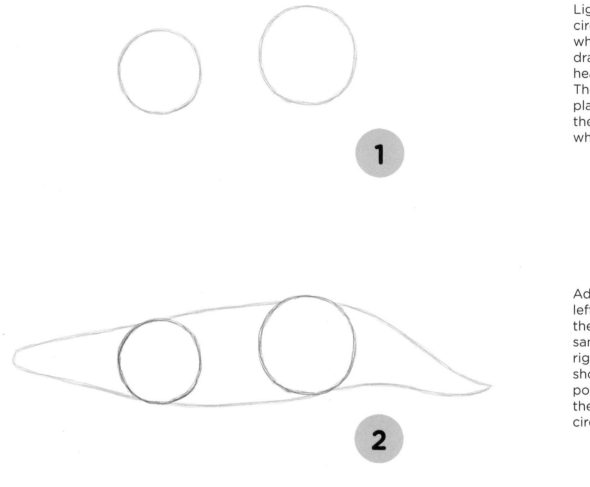

1

Lightly sketch two circles on your paper, which will help you draw the body and head in the next step. The farther apart you place these circles, the longer the whale's body will be.

2

Add an arc on the left as a guide for the head. Do the same thing on the right, but the shape should end in a point. Then connect the two original circles with lines.

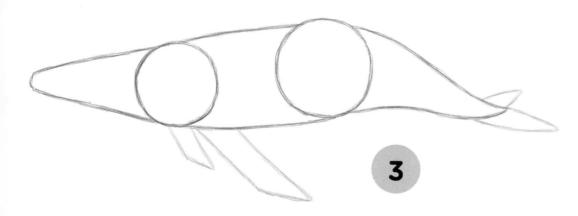

3

Complete your initial guide lines by adding the flippers and flukes. Make sure your guides look proportional before moving on to the next step.

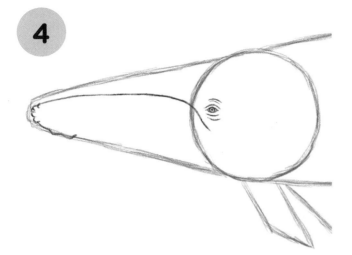

4

Draw a tiny football shape for the eye and add a circle inside for the actual eyeball. Add some curved lines above and below the eye for creases on the skin. Then add the lower part of the mouth with a long, curved line and a bumpy lip.

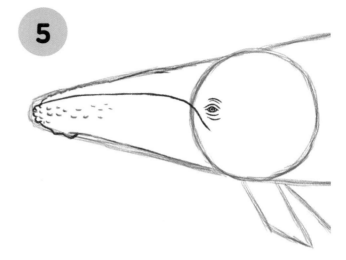

5

Darken the top part of the initial arc with bumps and waves. Draw an extra curved bump and a short line below it for the blowhole. Then finish the lower part of the mouth and add a few lines for the bumpy detail.

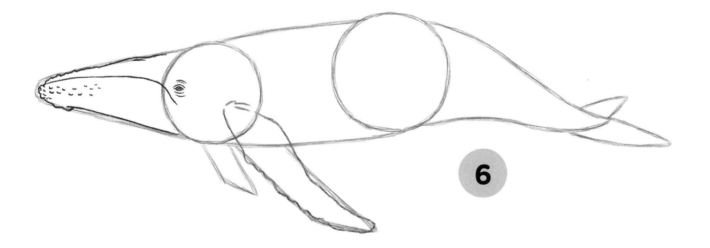

6

Use the big, angular shape under the body as a guide to draw the first flipper. As you darken the guide lines, make the left edge wavy and the tip rounder. Stretch the top of the flipper up into the shape of the body and add a couple of extra lines for detail.

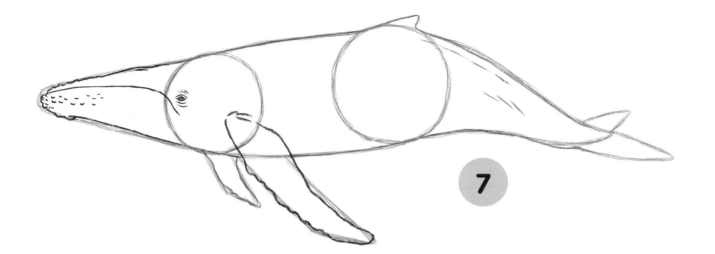

Draw the main part of the body. At the top of the second initial circle, draw the short dorsal fin on the back, and on the bottom, make sure not to overlap the flipper that's on this side of the body. Then draw the flipper on the other side of the body.

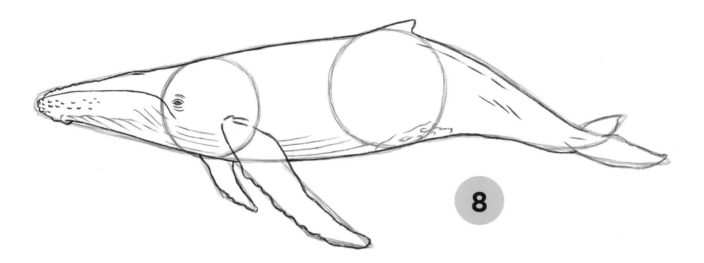

Use the triangular shapes on the right to draw the tail. Make the shapes rounder and use some wavy lines for an organic feel. Then add a few more lines and shapes within the body for extra detail. Don't draw too many lines; just add a few for texture.

SHADING FOR DIMENSION After putting down value to represent the whale's color, add some shading to make your drawing look three-dimensional. To do this, add shadows to the underside of the whale's body, even where it is white. This should make it look like the light is hitting the whale on the top and that it has a shadow underneath. To get light and dark values, vary the pressure on your pencil. Be sure to shade lightly at first, and then gradually build up to the level of darkness that you like.

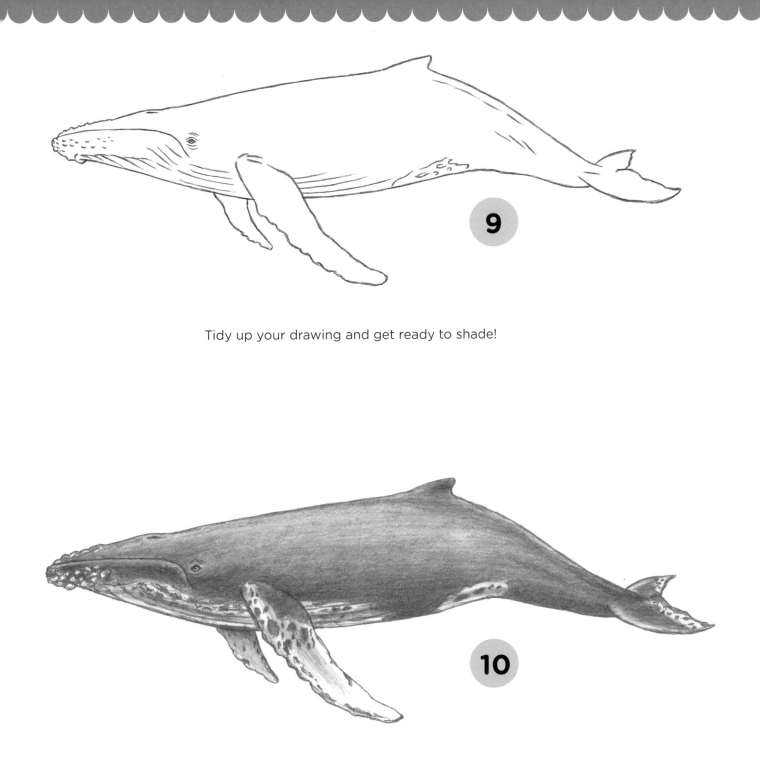

Tidy up your drawing and get ready to shade!

Add a medium value to most of the body with long, smooth, horizontal strokes for a sleek surface. Avoid a rough and gritty texture. Leave a few blank to represent white, including the circular shapes on the tip of the mouth, the ridges at the bottom, and the flippers and tail. Then add some splotchy markings in some of these areas. Then add some shading to give the form dimension and volume.

STINGRAY

1

Sketch a big circle as a guide for the main part of the stingray's body.

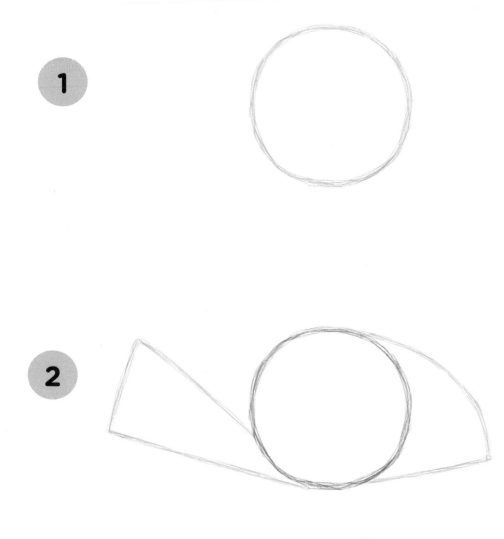

2

On the left side of the circle, draw a triangle-like shape as a guide for the first wing. On the right, complete the guide for the head using a curved line and a straight line.

3

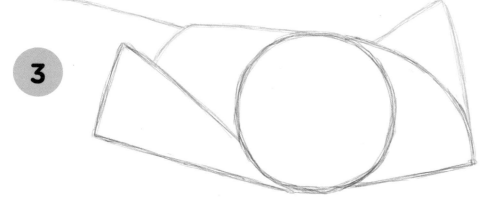

Draw two more triangle-like shapes and a line to finish up the guides for the stingray.

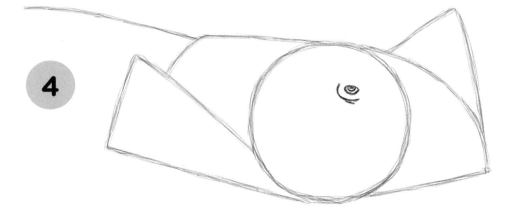

4

Sketch in the eye and add the pupil. Draw a couple of curved lines under the eye to give some structure to the eye area.

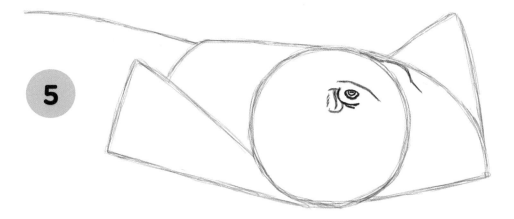

5

To the left of the eye, draw a couple of curved lines for the respiratory opening called a spiracle. Then draw a curved line above the eye to create a thick brow, and add the brow for the eye on the other side of the head. The other eye isn't visible from this angle.

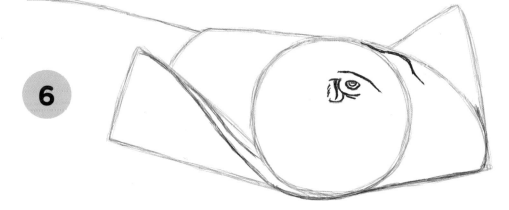

6 Darken the front part of the guides but make the lines a bit curvier.

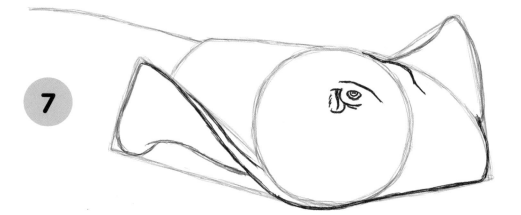

7 Draw the pectoral fins using the triangle guides on the sides. The bottom of the wing should curve up higher than the guide and have a folded appearance.

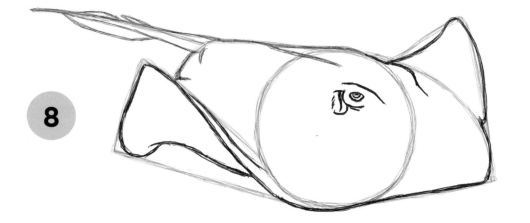

8 Create the rest of the stingray's body and add an extra line at the top for a ridge. Complete the tail, making the base thick and the tip pointy. On the top edge of the tail, draw a short, thin, pointy shape for the stinging spine.

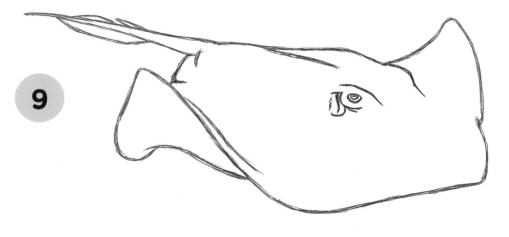

9

Clean up your drawing by erasing the guide lines that you no longer need.

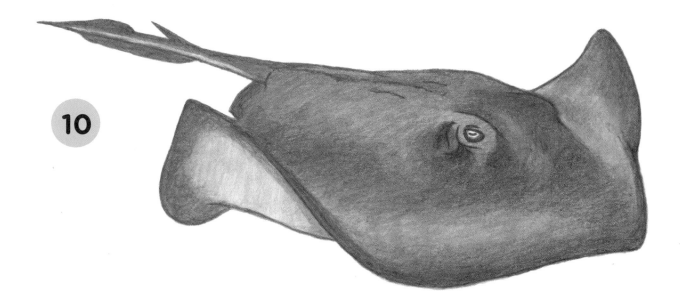

10

Some stingrays have patterns on their bodies, but for a common stingray like this one, just add an even medium value all over. Don't shade the inside of the eye, and leave the bottom of the fin and a line on the tail a lighter value. Add darker value around the head and along the edges to give the body more structure. Continue to gradually add a darker value throughout the body until you're happy with the result.

MOORISH IDOL

1

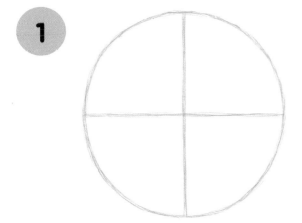

Draw a big circle as a guide for the main part of the body. Then draw a vertical line and a horizontal line intersecting the middle of the circle. These are construction lines that will help you place the Moorish idol's features.

2

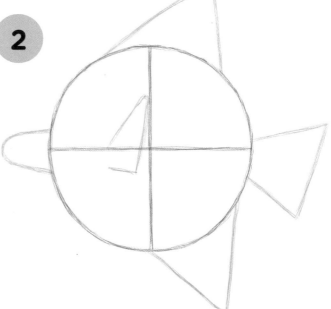

Draw the guide for the mouth on the left side. Then use triangular shapes for the fins and tail.

3

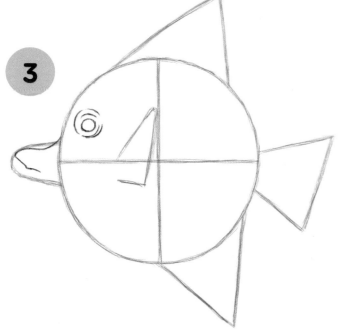

Lightly sketch a small circle for the eye and add a few curved lines around it for detail. Then use the small arc on the left as a guide to draw the top part of the mouth.

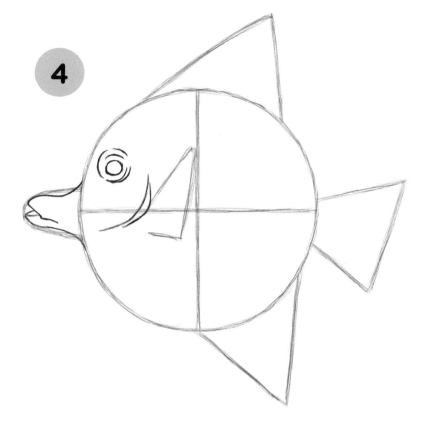

4

Darken the bottom part of the mouth to create the lower jaw. Add a small, curved line on the lower jaw for the open mouth. Two long, curved lines make the gill covers.

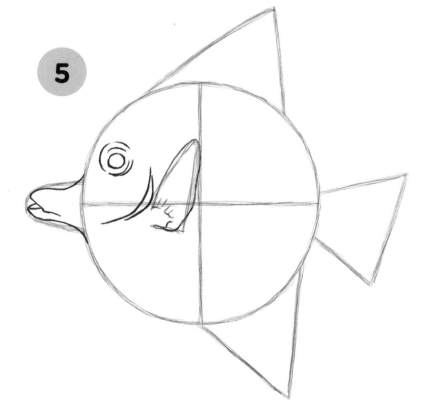

5

Use the triangle-like shape in the middle of the body as a guide to draw the pectoral fin. Add some detail lines at the base of the fin.

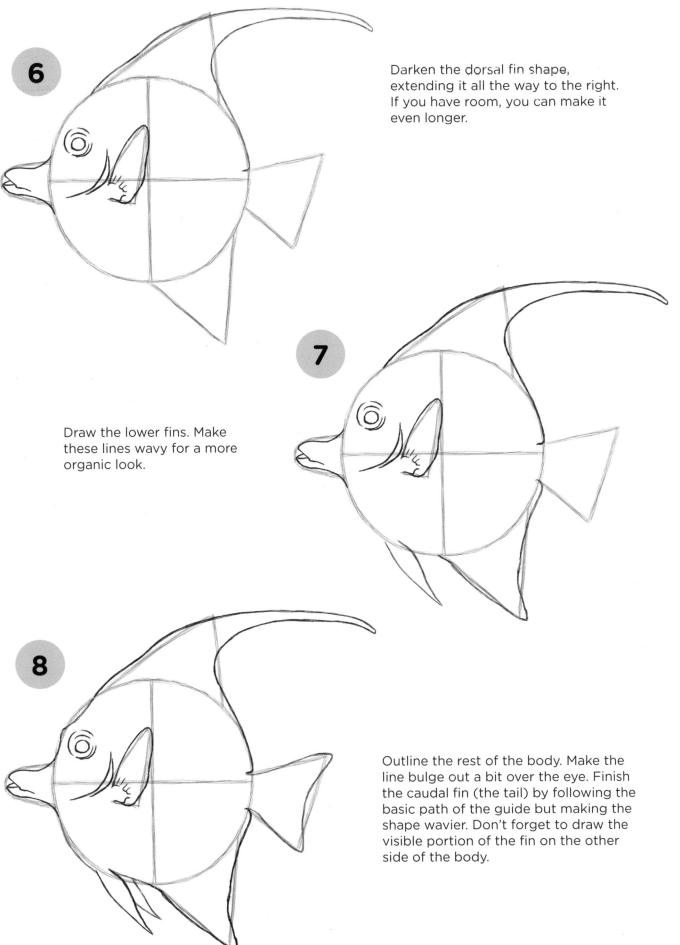

6

Darken the dorsal fin shape, extending it all the way to the right. If you have room, you can make it even longer.

7

Draw the lower fins. Make these lines wavy for a more organic look.

8

Outline the rest of the body. Make the line bulge out a bit over the eye. Finish the caudal fin (the tail) by following the basic path of the guide but making the shape wavier. Don't forget to draw the visible portion of the fin on the other side of the body.

9

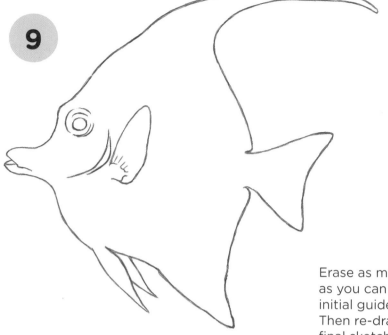

Erase as much as you can of the initial guide lines. Then re-draw any final sketch lines you'd like to fix.

ANATOMY KNOWLEDGE
Most fish have the same general anatomy. There is the head, body, and tail. On this Moorish idol drawing, you can see the gill cover, the pectoral fin behind the gills, the dorsal fin on the top, the tail fin, and the fins on the bottom of the body. Take a look at a similar-looking fish to the Moorish idol, such as the freshwater angelfish, and note the differences in all of these structures. Try drawing an angelfish now that you've drawn the Moorish idol to test your powers of observation.

10

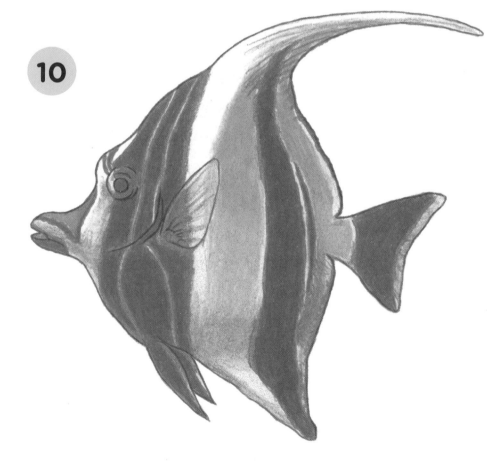

Add some shading to your Moorish idol to give it dimension and volume, especially near the bottom of the body. These fish have vertical stripes on their bodies, so add the value accordingly, starting with a light pressure and slowly building up to the level of darkness you want. The pectoral fin is transparent. To get this effect, just follow the path of the stripe and shade the fin lightly.

SEA TURTLE

1

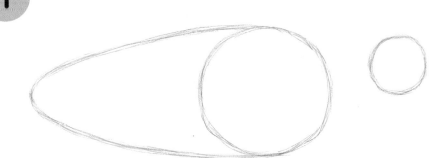

Lightly sketch two circles and a big arc for guides. The shape on the left will be the shell, and the small circle on the right will help you draw the head. Don't place the oval too far to the right or the turtle's neck will end up too long.

2

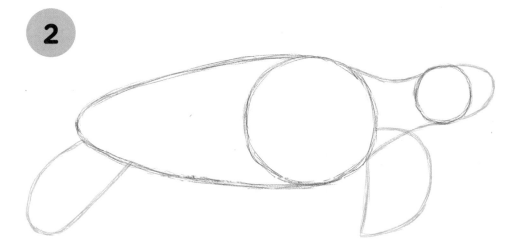

Connect the head to the shell to form the guide for the neck. Add an arc for the front part of the face, and two shapes for the flipper-like legs.

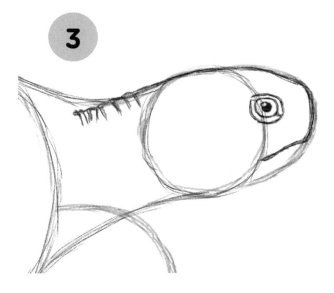

3

Draw the eye and a couple of lines surrounding the eye for extra detail. Then create the line for the top of the head, which includes the top of the mouth and the skin folds on the neck.

4

Draw the chin and the rest of the head, including additional lines on the neck.

5

Use the shapes under the body to draw the flippers. Follow the basic paths of the arcs, making the left sides wavy.

6

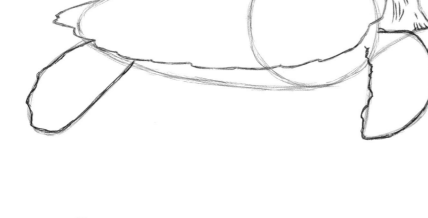

To draw the top half of the shell, follow the path of the top guide line. For the bottom edge of the shape, add small, slightly arched lines instead of a single long line.

7

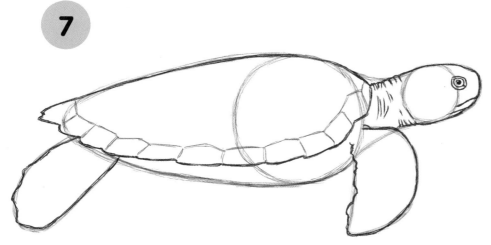

Begin to add the shapes along the bottom of the top shell. They can be square-like or pentagon-like. Darken the bottom part of the body simply by following the initial guide.

8

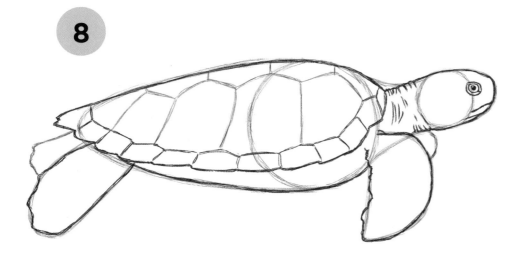

Now add larger pentagon-like shapes on the top of the shell and small vertical lines at the top. Then add the flippers on the other side of the body.

9

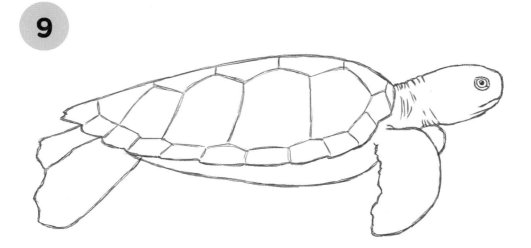

For a cleaner look, erase as much of you can of the initial guide lines. Don't worry about erasing all of the guides. It's okay to leave some behind. Also re-draw any final sketch lines that you may have accidentally erased.

10

Add some shading to give your sea turtle more dimension and volume. Then create the dark spots on the head and fins and shade them in. The spots on the edges of the flippers are bigger, and they get smaller closer to the center. Add lighter value to the rest of your drawing. Use an even value on the shell for a smooth finish or an uneven value for an older, worn-down look.

OCTOPUS

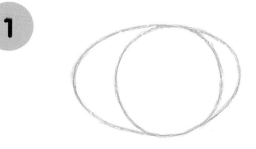

1 Begin by sketching a circle with an arc on either side. Leave enough room for the tentacles on the left side.

2 Add the guide for the lower half of the body, as well as two tentacles.

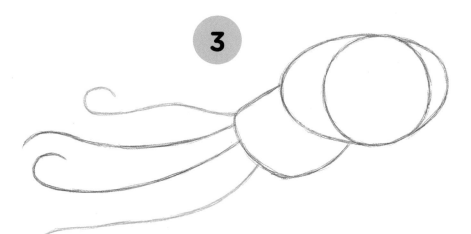

3 Add two more lines to the left of the body for two more tentacles. Don't make them all the same or too straight. Wavy lines and a couple of curved tips will make your drawing look more organic.

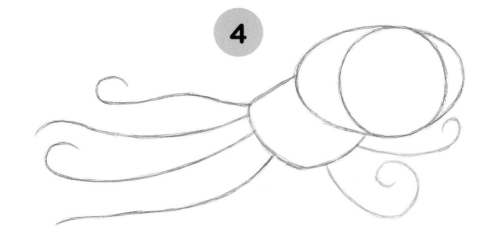

4

Draw a couple more lines on the right side of the body for more tentacles. There are eight tentacles on an octopus, but stop drawing guide lines here. You can use the other tentacles as guides when drawing the remaining two.

Draw an oval eye with a small rectangular shape inside for the pupil. A semi-circular bumpy line around the eye creates the fleshy structure that surrounds it. Draw another wavy line for the eye on the other side.

5

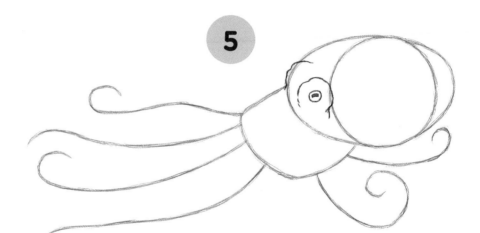

6

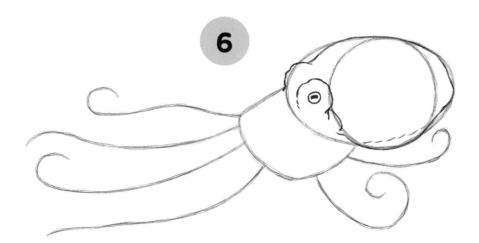

Use the initial guides to draw the rest of the mantle, and add a dotted line along the bottom.

7

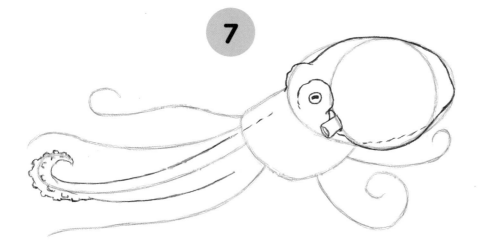

Below the eye, draw the siphon, which looks similar to a cylinder. Then draw the first tentacle. Darken your sketch lines when you get the shape right. Add curved lines for suction cups. These are on the underside of the curved tentacle.

8

Draw the tentacles above and below the one you just drew. Make the bases thick and the tips thin. Remember that wavy lines will look more organic. There are no suction cups visible on these tentacles.

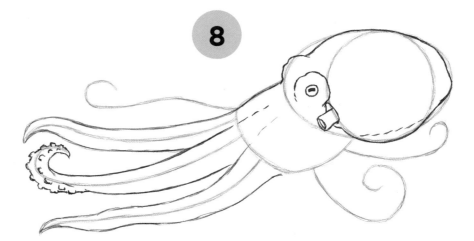

9

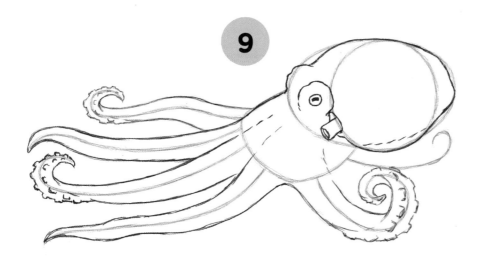

Draw two more tentacles, including suction cups on the undersides. Octopuses have two rows of suction cups per tentacle.

10

There is one more tentacle guide line, but draw three more in this step. Some lines will overlap, and much of these remaining tentacles won't be visible.

SIMPLIFYING Even though octopuses have eight tentacles, you don't need to draw all eight; several could be hiding behind the body and not visible from this angle.

Tidy up your drawing to get it ready for shading!

11

Add some shading to your drawing to give it more dimension and volume. Because the octopus is on the ocean floor, the shadows will be mainly near the bottom. Add a medium value all over the body smoothly and avoid a rough, gritty texture.

12

ORCA

Sketch a big circle near the middle of the paper as a guide for the body. Add a smaller circle on the top-right side for the head. Don't draw the circles too close together, otherwise your orca will end up too short.

Add a curved line on the head circle. Then connect the head to the body circle and add two more long lines under the big circle to create the guide for the lower part of the body.

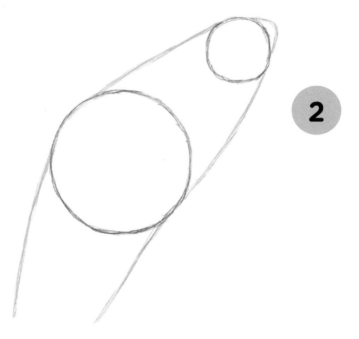

Finish up your guides by adding the dorsal fin, two pectoral fins, and a long, horizontal line at the bottom for the surface of the water.

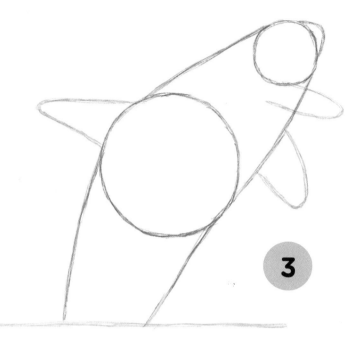

3

4

Draw the eye, but don't worry too much about it, as it will basically get lost when you shade later. Then use the arc as a guide to draw the mouth and complete the head shape.

5

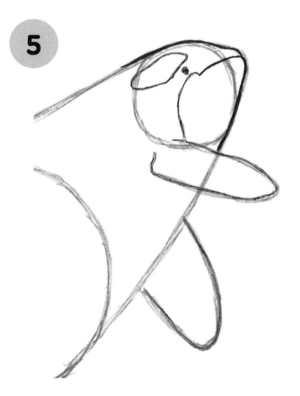

Inside the head, draw a shape above the eye. Make a line that goes from the mouth down toward the flipper to indicate where the separation of color will be. Then darken the flipper shapes.

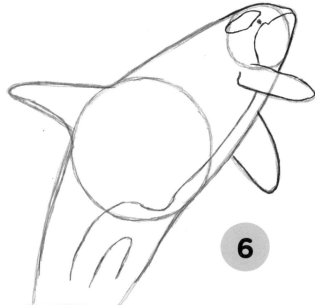

As you darken the dorsal fin, make the bottom curvier so that it is a bit thinner. Then finish up the body, taking care not to overlap the top flipper or dorsal fin. Finally, draw a series of lines inside the body for the color separation.

6

Finalize the water surface with a rough horizontal line. Then begin to draw the splashing water. It doesn't have to look exactly like this drawing, and it's okay if the lines overlap the body. Add tiny circles and ovals to represent water droplets.

7

8

Finish the water dripping from the orca on the right side. As long as they're wavy and sort of U-shaped, they should be just fine. Just don't add too many, or it will start to look crowded. Add some of these wavy lines inside the orca's flipper too.

9

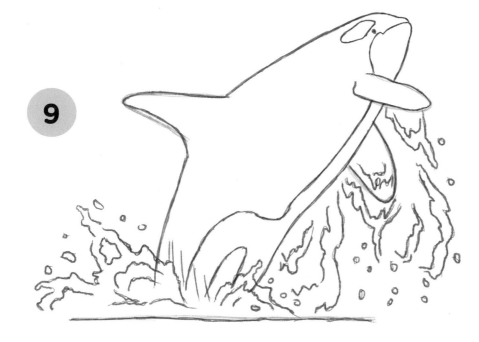

Clean up your drawing and get ready to shade!

10

Use a dark value on the body except for the underside, the patch of white on the head, a wavy shape below the dorsal fin called the saddle, and a section in the middle for shine. Leave some small circles blank for drops of water. Then add alternating dark and medium values to the water to create ripples and shadows. Use a medium value for the splashing water but leave the wavy lines white for foam. Finally, add a medium value to the underside of the body for a shadow.

ABOUT THE AUTHOR

How2DrawAnimals.com teaches beginning artists how to draw all kinds of animals from A to Z through video demonstrations and simple step-by-step instructions. Started in 2012 by an animal-loving artist with a bachelor's degree in illustration, How2DrawAnimals offers a new tutorial each week and now boasts hundreds of animal drawing tutorials. Working in graphite and in colored pencils, and in both realistic and cartoon styles, How2DrawAnimals has featured animals from all letters of the alphabet, from Aardvark to Zebra and everything in between. See more at How2DrawAnimals.com.

ALSO IN THE LET'S DRAW SERIES:

Let's Draw Cats
ISBN: 978-0-7603-8070-3

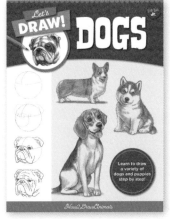

Let's Draw Dogs
ISBN: 978-0-7603-8072-7

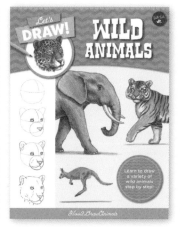

Let's Draw Favorite Animals
ISBN: 978-0-7603-8074-1

Let's Draw Wild Animals
ISBN: 978-0-7603-8076-5

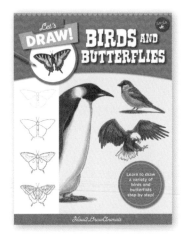

Let's Draw Birds & Butterflies
ISBN: 978-0-7603-8078-9

Let's Draw Dinosaurs
ISBN: 978-0-7603-8082-6

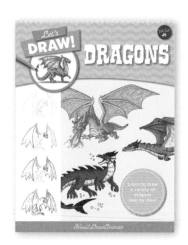

Let's Draw Dragons
ISBN: 978-0-7603-8084-0

The Quarto Group

Inspiring | Educating | Creating | Entertaining

www.WalterFoster.com